DISCIPLINE YOUR DREAMS

VAISHNAVI RAMESH

DEDICATION

*This book is for the ones who have known
that dreams do not flourish in chaos,
but in clarity, shaped by focus and self-belief.*

*To those who have dared to dream
not just in sleep, but in waking moments of stillness.*

*May these words remind you
that reflection is a form of strength,
and discipline is not a cage
but the path that makes your dreams real.*

With deep gratitude,

VAISHNAVI RAMESH

Contents

Contents

Contents

Preface

In an age of instant gratification, fleeting trends, and constant distractions, the quiet strength of discipline often goes unnoticed. Yet, it is this very discipline that separates intention from achievement and desire from action. This book was born from a simple, yet powerful realization: success whether personal, professional, or spiritual is not the result of luck or talent alone, but of consistent, focused effort over time.

Self-development is not a destination; it is a lifelong journey. It demands courage to face one's limitations, clarity to set meaningful goals, and the resilience to grow through setbacks. At the heart of this journey lies discipline

Whether you are just beginning your journey of self-improvement or seeking to deepen your practice, may this book serve as a guide, a challenge, and a companion on the road to becoming the best version of yourself.

1. DREAMS

What are dreams?

Are dreams the only scenes experienced when human sleeps?

Or dreams, the scenes that human yearns for?

Slumbering between the past and future.

Only prioritizing the wounds and wishes of human life.

Dictating one's own emotional and mental essence.

Revolving around the realm of the known.

Dreams are emotional accumulation beneath the sheath of the mind.

Never crossing the limitations of human thought.

Unable to dive into the ocean of human intelligence.

The ultimate truth has been hidden for ages.

And each human explores at different stages.

"Life being the ultimate dream in reality."

Extending into the realm of thoughts.

Unlocking infinite possibilities, residing now and then.

Let's explore the depths of human understanding!

2. HUMAN UNDERSTANDING

"Humans" the most advanced creatures on Earth,
Depending upon their innate nature of birth.
Shall trail the paths of their ancestors ahead.
Learning and revolving around a limited sphere.
At a certain age, as their knowledge spurns;
Pushing them into the reality of life.
Experimenting and breaking all the boundaries built.
As thoughts differ, boundaries evolve;
As thoughts unite, boundaries devolve.
The ultimate understanding of humans,
Depends merely upon their surroundings.
Random exposure to the thick and thin.
Helps to get away from the knowledge brim.
Diving ahead into the oceanic kin.
Shall ignite the source of "The Self" within!

3. THE ATTENTION

"The attention and care make the whole difference!"
The things that attract your attention, accumulate the most.
The things that you love, pile around you.
Your thoughts being the source of the connection loop.
What all you think, you attract!
When you think and yearn for good,
All good things seem to happen around you.
When your thoughts are filled with doubt and fear,
The castle of darkness arises within you.
It is you who designs your inner castle!
Options being plenty and there is no point of nil.
Same with the thoughts that flow within you.
As a thought of a person triggers your mental string,
The tension on the string spoils the rhythmic cling,
Making you travel into a dilemmatic spring.
Where nothing seems fair as you wished so far.
Where does this all start afar?
It all started with your thoughts!
Attention to your thoughts escalates your path.
And you begin to design your inner castle as you wished so far!

4. THE MENTAL STRING

Thoughts the beads of your mental string.
From where the rhythm of life begins.
As you are aware of your own thoughts.
You will travel alive so far.
As you tune into the harmonious tune within.
Enlightens the hidden rhythm of life.
As you begin to merge with the flow of life.
Unaware of the rocks beside.
Just as the water flows ahead,
Beyond all the stones and shrubs.
Life moves on, with a gentle flow.
Bending smoothly over the twists and turns.
Making the voyage a complete fun.
With gratification over and over again!

5. UNAWARENESS

As you are unaware of the thoughts, constantly churning your
heart,
Your inner world agitates with burn.
No clue of things happening around,
Every action seemingly wrong.
The haste of life spinning unknown.
Clutters piling all around.
Annoying, where did all things begin from?
Leading into such a dark regime.
Is there any way out of this hell?
The chase begins as your spine chills.
The time when questions flood over and over,
The point of unawareness is over.
And it's time to embark the journey of life.
With awareness filling your heart inside!

6. ONCE YOU START QUESTIONING

Once you start questioning vehemently,
You have arrived on the spot!
The spot where your life turns AHEAD.
Opening into infinite possibilities and opportunities.
Now it is time to choose your way.
After a long tired path,
Rushing thoughts draining all way long,
Finally onto the way of light.
The light that envisions your mind with clarity ahead.
At once you start to question yourself,
Instead of blaming and reasoning others.
For all the blunders that had happened to you.
You enter into the point of introspection,
Where you deeply connect to your inner version!

7. UNSTOPPABLE CHATTER

You hear an unstoppable chatter, travelling all way;
Echoing for years and decades along the way.
Wherever you go, with whomever you are;
It keeps on murmuring you, the right and wrong.
Reflecting based on the mental theories known so far.
Clinging and swinging over to the moments of your life,
Framing things good and bad, but nothing being sure!
Is that the voice of your inner self?
Or just a broken record?
Looping over and over the same pattern of life.
Resonating to the boring, judgmental tune;
Reasoning and labelling all things, from a single point of view;
The point of view from where, no other scenes are aware.
Only endlessly chattering and reasoning.
But at once as your introspection starts,
It is time for all the chatters to stop!

8. INTROSPECTION

INTROSPECTION an act of looking inward.
Into the roots where all emotions stir.
Whatever may be the emotional terms;
Glad or sad, creative or depressed, confident or doubtful;
Furious or frustrated, focused or lost, dynamic or livid.
The moment you are aware of your given life,
You step into the world of your inner Self.
Into the journey of the unknown sphere,
Where all things seem elite.
Onto the journey of exploring yourself,
And your inner unknown potential of the Self.
Getting out of the loop of reason and blame.
You enter into the vast space of fame,
Where your dreams align as your thoughts ascend.
Stepping ahead from a chaotic space into a state of flux!

9. ALL YOUR QUESTIONS ANSWERED

Entering into the sphere of your inner world,
After all those endless chatters freeze,
Here you are aware of your own Self.
Your awareness being the central stream of life,
"What you are aware is where you lie."
As you are aware of your own breath,
You transcend mental patterns ahead,
Surpassing the mysteries of mind.
Mind being rigid for ages, now calms down at various stages,
Revealing you, your infinite potential;
To overcome all the unwanted clutters and live life to the fullest.
The perfect state where all the questions answer is gained,
Is the place of the listener's throne.
Where silence fills with full of answers alone!

10. THE POWER OF LISTENING

The power of listening immerses you in the present.
As you listen, your awareness peaks.
Listening to the different tunes of life,
You abide by Nature's rhythm alive.
Listening shall calm down your rushing nerves,
Descending your infinite thoughts beside.
Igniting the stream of awareness within;
Just like a music swaying away, a million hearts aside,
It's through the art of listening, the energy surpasses abide.
Making wonders flutter around you,
Into the natural rhythm of life.
As you listen to the chirping of the birds;
The crashing of the waves;
The blowing of the wind;
The rustling of the trees;
Even the sound of your breath.
Every sound you listen, stretches you into deep silence.
Magically tuning your heart's rhythm, to the source!

11. TUNE OF YOUR HEART

The tune of your heart being the inner gateway,
Any decision to be taken;
Listen to your heart!
It flawlessly guides you to the perfect way.
As your heart throbs, set things aside,
Let it calm down, take a pause as you freeze.
A rushing heart is a sign of grief,
As your mind hears a melancholic tune,
Loaded with hardships and sufferings, ruin.
The natural rhythm of the heart's stream.
As your beat calms down, you feel alight;
To take all decisions clear and right.
Listen to your heart!
Your heart knows you,
And guides you at all times from now!

12. THE DECISION

Whenever you decide, a duality arise.
A clash between your heart and brain.
As you listen to your brain, it trains your mind,
To stick on to the knowledge as far known.
As you listen to your heart, you travel afar.
Beyond the limitations of mind; so far,
Things begin to happen at random pace,
With no hint of rush to its rhythmic phase.
Believe in your heart!
All things might reveal,
The hidden secrets of the unknown world.

13. PERFECT TIMING

Everything happens in perfect timing!
Have you ever wondered, how timing works?
From the systematic movement of the planet Earth;
To the sun rising with perfect glare.
From the limited movement of the tides in ocean,
To the tremendous transformation of a seed into a tree.
Everything happens in perfect timing!
So as things happening to you,
Falls at places in perfect timing.
All your desires will come true,
Wait patiently for the perfect timing, as things mature!
Timing is hidden within you!
Believe your inner potential for sure!

14. TIME IS NOWHERE, TIME IS NOW HERE

"Time is nowhere, Time is now here."
The moment you start to believe in yourself,
Things begin to change rapidly,
Things once annoyed now settle down,
To a pleasing note of silencing calm.
The universal truth of ages, passed down by different sages,
You become what you believe!
Experimenting with your beliefs, shall define the pattern of life.
Belief, the foundation of every human invention.
Embedding the seed of all innovation.
Your thoughts are your beliefs!
Condition and organize your thoughts,
To transform your beliefs afar.
And your mind expands into the reality of abundance.
For life is the only chance to explore one's infinite inner strength.
Explore the game of life, framing your beliefs ahead.

15. MONITOR YOUR THOUGHTS

Thoughts flow in abundance!
At once, you are awake in the morning sun!
Thoughts flood over and over,
Even as you do things in order.
Running life in autopilot mode,
From refreshing to grooming and off to work.
Do we monitor all thoughts that flash in our minds?
The reality unveils when you pause and watch,
Your mental scenes flooding so far.
Pausing allows you to slow down your pace,
When a few little things astonish your days.
Awareness being the center of attention.
As you are aware of your mental space,
Your energy stays secured in a finite place.

16. AS YOU SLOW, MORE SPACE IS CLEARED

As you slow down the pace of your daily life,
More space is cleared on your mental slide.
By watching your thoughts flow aside,
Centering your mind deep inside.
You enter into a vivid field, where numerous possibilities are
revealed.
Embedded within are the seeds of creativity.
You explore more unique ways to lead your life in the systematic
race.
Completely free from the doubtful phase.
That often triggers a mental chase.
All things begin to happen at a random swing.
The moment you begin, to count all your blessings.
Your eyes would truly witness the evident life,
That you are blessed with and experiencing alive!

17. VALUES BUILD YOU

As you begin to witness the flow of your life,
You will start exploring great heights.
As you deeply focus on the values of your life,
You build a strong empire inside.
"Values are the escorts of life."
Onwards the journey, your mission, enlight.
Excavating you into the unknown spheres,
Deep into the roots truth secure.
From kindness, patience, empathy, compassion and honesty;
To forgiveness, gratitude, learning, innovation and responsibility.
The list goes on and on.
Grab on to your own values at arm.
As they are the only post guards of your life!

18. GRATITUDE

Values mark the typical milestones ahead,
"GRATITUDE" acts as an inner cleansing agent;
Cleanses and nourishes your factory of thoughts,
And fills your heart with valuable spots.
Your perception of the world changes;
As you travel on the path of gratitude for ages.
Start with a habit of thanking for the little things in life,
The list expands widely, as the momentary thanking arise,
Happiness fills your heart.
A feeling of content nourishing your mind.
Enabling you to love and share things with all.
Sharing builds caring, nurturing emotional integration,
Revealing the nature's significant fact that, "All are under a
single roof!"

19. NATURE'S INTELLIGENCE

Humans replicate Nature's intelligence.
Nature's intelligence shaping human innovations.
Technologies evolve mimicking Nature's process.
The planes inspired by the flight of birds;
Bullet trains by the beak of a bird;
Drones flying like the buzzing bees.
Admiration fills from every end of Nature's wheel.
Intelligence without brains, the natural hymn.
Intuition, adaptation in harmony align.
Just like a leaf of the lotus repelling water,
Our mind should repel the unwanted thoughts that block our
way.
With Nature's intelligence guiding all the way!

20. CONNECT WITH NATURE FOR SOLUTION

Whenever your stuck connect with Nature for luck.
Listen to the silent whispers of nature,
And step ahead to create your signature.
Nature the best teacher for ages;
Preaches you lessons at different stages.
Spending time with nature,
Reveals its systematic features!
Never rush for your answers,
Just observe the pattern of connection.
As you slow down, you go deep beyond;
Into accurate detailing that stands still.
Nature has already solved all your questions.
The solutions you seek, are just looping around;
In the silent spaces between you and the Nature !

21. THE LESSONS THAT SEASONS TEACH

Everything changes as seasons come and go!
Seasons unveil the rhythmic pattern of Nature.
As petals bloom and swing in spring;
New ideas emerge deep within.
Plant few ideas on the season, spring!
As the summer brings bright sunshine within;
Days get longer, as we act and thrive.
On expansion, the fruits of labour arrive!
Autumn comes, the harvest done;
It's time to reflect and let go of things, undone.
Though the leaves wither, the trees stand still.
Trusting in the process, releasing with grace!
Winter follows, and the world gets quiet.
It's time to go on an inward ride.
When rest reflects and restores inside;
The sacred renewal brings new transformation on all sides.
Seasons align with the rhythms of the Earth;
Whispering the fact, "Change is permanent by birth!"

22. RESILIENCE OF A GRASS

Though crushed under the foot,
Or flattened by a fierce storm,
A grass never loses its form.
Even after numerous trims and cuts,
Recovers with grace afresh.
Growing back to its original state,
Again and again, without resisting change.
Teaching us the survival trick,
Of when to stand and bend.
Everywhere it's found,
From the garden to the highways,
In the playgrounds and battlefields.
Once rooted, it simply grows,
Trusting Earth's process on the flow.
Conveying one strong message;
The power of resilience, to get back up after every fall.
The fall is not the end, only a bend!

23. LIFE IS A PERFECT BALANCE

The light of the sun,

Shade of the tree,

Stillness after a storm,

Everything stays balanced in Nature, prolong.

The human emotions, as well,

You learn from the failures,

That trains you for success.

You receive when you give.

You control your bests, surrender the rests.

Life is a perfect balance in harmony.

Not pushing too hard or resisting too far.

Amidst all the ups and downs,

There is a centering point.

Balancing your heart and leading your path!

24. DISCIPLINE YOUR DREAMS

DISCIPLINE the silent architect behind every fulfilled dream.
As the heart beholds your dream, discipline makes you reach the realm.
Ignite your dreams with the power of habits.
The light shall glow and enlighten the world.
A dream without discipline is just a wind's blow.
Discipline a perfect devotion with patience.
Discipline the art of structuring your dream.
Inspiring and transforming you within,
Onto the path of your mission with an intentional vision.
Practice builds boundaries that secure your dreams.
As your purpose revealed, your journey ever fueled within!

25. EVERY YEAR YOU GROW

Birthdays celebrated year after year.
With pleasant surprises and dreams wished ahead.
Candles blown off, after a secret wishing inside.
Have you ever wondered why?
The trail being followed blindly wide.
Instead, light a candle after your desired wish.
And watch its glow as it flicks.
Your wishes come true with a bright start of hue.
As you watch the spark dancing for you.
Birthdays are gentle reminders, reminding our journey is a gift.
And whispers from the universe to keep ever blooming with
SMILE lit!

26. GLOOM AND BLOOM

Every gloom carries a seed to bloom.
Gloom teaches patience,
As bloom appears in time.
Gloom doesn't deny any boon,
It paves the way for it to grow and bloom.
A flower blooms to its fullest when its time arrives.
Every gloomy situation preaches to wait with patience.
Only as the roots get coiled, they stay centered at a place.
Human emotions get coiled to strengthen their base.
As you ache, you finally awake after all those tiring days!

27. AWAKE AND AWAKEN

AWAKE, the conscious state,
AWAKEN, the stirring of the soul.
Once you are awake, you are aware of your state;
Protruding away from sleep, you start to notice the world at
stake.
Awakening the pure awareness, routing you to the center within.
As light awakens your eyes, truth awakens your consciousness.
Awake being the spark and awakening the fire.
As you listen deeper, you are tuned to live higher.
As your breath becomes your empire!

28. BREATH BECOMES YOUR GUIDE

When the mind races, the vision blurs.
As you rush in haze, you misjudge every gaze.
Breath being an anchor, every voyager yearns.
When chaos strikes, your breath becomes spiked.
Just take a pause and breathe.
Breath flows in the present, relieving grief.
The silence in breath shattering the mental noise.
The flow of your breath, an armor unique.
Vanishing the invisible barrier between your fear and power.
You gather strength as you inhale;
And release the stress built as you exhale.
Just follow your breath!
Your breath never lies but only tells,
The route to the secret valley yet to explore within oneself!

29. THE INWARD JOURNEY

"SELF EXPLORATION" the inward journey,
One long journey from the mind to the heart.
Life being a puzzle so far;
Stepping onto exploration, shall reveal the mystic path.
Life, a beautiful landscape to watch.
Getting deeper into the roots to discover the paths.
Where you find yourself apart from the thoughts.
As you descend down the steep knowledge rocks.
Onto the shore where stillness speaks louder in silence.
Exploration begins with a simple questioning,
Of the roles that you play day to day,
The only way to solve the mystery of life?
Reflecting and directing the mind to the source within.
You travel in the present, where you unmask and unfold!

30. THE PATH OF MIND TO HEART

When your mind carries the questions, your heart bears all the
answers.
Mind the servant of the heart.
Carrying the map of life and the heart serving, compass straight.
Mind preaches control, where the heart preaches to connect.
When the mind figures out wrong and right;
Heart whispers the truth delight.
While the mind understands the pattern of life;
The heart reveals its meaning upright.
As your mind stays, your heart feels.
Listen to them as they both teach.
The coherent essence of life's stream.
Tune your mind to the rhythm of the heart,
To live a prosperous and fulfilled life across!

31. MONITOR AND DESIGN YOUR THOUGHTS

As you are aware of your mind,
You monitor and design your thoughts,
Becoming the architect of your inner world.
Thoughts flowing as a stream.
Evolving out of memory and perceptual screen.
Just watch as it slows, to direct its flow.
Without any judgment, observance on the go!
Mastering your thoughts is mastering your mind.
As your mind is filled with thoughts.
When your mind says "You can't",
Reprogram the same, with "I can".
Everything works like a miracle when you take a simple stand.
To monitor and observe your thoughts,
You design your inner world, which reflects the outer world !

32. REFLECTION IS IMPORTANT

Reflections the perfect remedies for all mental illnesses.
Also acting as a precaution, protecting us from dis-ease.
Cleaning up the mental space;
To pause, process and proceed.
Reflections the real mental warriors,
For inner harmony and peace!
Making invisible things visible;
Once the spot is caught, the healing starts.
Not to worry about the repeating thoughts.
As reflection makes you stare fearlessly at the odds.
A bold stare at your life that dares your heart,
To overcome the blocks that created chaos in your heart.
Creating a central space to respond and not to react.
Strengthening your true self.
As mistakes become lessons;
And scars pave the way to thrones in the present.
At last, a major shift from pain to purpose, gained!

33. BE THE CHANGE YOU DESIRE

BELIEVE in the version of your new self.
If you wish to change the world,
Then Dare to change yourself.
Be the change you desire to be!
Walk on the path of truth.
With little habits en route.
The change you desire starts within you.
Just a few small steps taken full-fledged.
Without waiting for time to make you shine.
The fire within you is alive anew.
To glow and share the light with the crew.
Don't wait too long to start your plan.
As you resist change, you let EGO play the game.
When you listen inward, you traverse beyond.
As the still silence guides you.
Walking through the meadows of your inner self.
You discover your new Self!

34. YOUR WORDS, TRUE MOTIVATION

True motivation is an inner job.

Though inspired from outside,

Staying on track is purely inside.

People may guide you but they can't walk for you.

You are the one who is going to walk on the path.

Mighty little steps shall unlock the secret way to the destination.

Your words being your only guide, true motivation inside.

Speak to yourself at times to refresh your thoughts align.

While everyone in the world is busy minding their own work.

As a bird is busy in search of its prey.

Or a spider persistently webbing for its stay.

Does a human teach the spider or the bird to do its work?

Every potential is packed inside its ownself.

Just in case, as for you,

The true search begins;

Only when your intentions are pristine !

35. THINK GOOD DO GOOD

As a man thinks, so is he.
As a man thinks, so he speaks.
As a man thinks, so he does.
As you start thinking good, you start doing good.
As you soften inside, you widen outside.
All your actions creating a ripple.
where strangers become friends without any clue.
Thoughts pave the way to actions.
Bringing thoughts into actions make you a vital being.
Every small action succeeds with a pure intention.
Look into your intentions as you build your own actions!

36. ACTIONS SPEAK LOUDER THAN WORDS

Words make promise, but only actions prove.
A seed holding silent the promise of a tree.
It shows only as it grows.
Growth is not about constant claiming of change.
The whole change doesn't happen in a day.
Though most good things well known to all,
Only a few practice them so far.
Apply all the known to tranform profound.
As you begin to live, you go deep inside your will.
Everything is achieved only through practice.
Like a seed sowed and watered with care.
A habit sowed should be practiced with care.
Habits refine and redefine your actions.
Making impossible things to happen.
Arising you closer to your dreams,
Practice makes your actions keen.

37. AS YOU LEARN YOU LEAD

As you learn to live, you lead others at will.
And the chain goes on, integrating the whole human will.
True leaders are not born; they truly transform.
As you find the light within you.
It sways away the darkness of the people around you.
Making their blurred vision, clear and visible.
As you are aware of your own truths.
It paves the way for others to pursue.
Your voice becomes subtle as your consciousness stands still.
Quite as a flame glowing steadily sane.
You live without chasing, dwelling in the flow.
You give without knowing, as you are in an abundant flow.
You cherish the depths of truth.
As the warmth spreads around.
You live your life with ease, spreading peace abound !

38. MASTERING YOUR SELF

Mastering your Self begins with pure understanding.
As you begin to understand yourself, you shall understand the
world.
Letting go of your knowns and welcoming the unknown.
Be aware of your patterns, triggers, strengths and spots that
blind.
Observe your thoughts and emotions without judgmental claims.
As you practice, you move into the phase of self-awareness
within.
Where you step into the field of mastering everything.
Discipline with devotion leads to mastering many things.
Cultivating patience, emotional flexibility begins.
The phrase "I KNOW ALL" ends your growth.
What you know is finite and the infinite yet unknown.
Though you master the known, still a student of the unknown.
As learning never ends!
As you accept uncertainty with utmost grace,
And let go of things, you cannot change.
Wisdom knocks your door and embraces alore!

39. BALANCING THE ART OF LIFE

Life is not a problem to solve.

But a spontaneous ride afar.

You have the freedom to choose from the options around.

Opposites clinging in perfect balancing sound.

Like the days after nights, success after failures,

Rest after work, motion behind every stillness.

Life is a beautiful picture.

Painted on the canvas of time.

Your dreams refine the picture.

Every stroke of your actions defined.

Adding detail to your reactions as you respond over time.

You are your very own masterpiece, untold!

40. LET GO, HOLD ON

Let go of your EGO and hold on to your GOAL,
A life without a goal is like a ship without a compass,
May sail and float, the destination remains untouched.
Life without a goal, an anchor without purpose.
Either big or small, goals redefine you.
Goals transform your days intentionally,
Shaping your time, shifting actions into progress.
Goal keeps you alive, letting go of your ego;
Bringing sunshine into your life.
As you shed your ego, you travel to your goal.
The only way to let your ego go,
Is to surrender to the greater power.
Which reminds you constantly,
That you're just a part of this vast Nature!

41. MAKE A PLAN TO ACHIEVE

Few little things planned and done, gives you great strength.
Igniting an innate connection within.
Building will power and empowers at keen.
As vague plans end up in vague days.
Discover your purpose so your energy never drains!
Read few quotes and feed your mind.
As your brain refreshes with this simple bolt.
Small beginnings welcome great endings.
Discovering your why's shall lead your way.
Beginning with inner clarity.
Your mind builds focus on what you fix.
Be the master of your mind and not a slave.
By building a mental routine as you structure your day.
Your brain is a mere muscle;
The more you use, the more flexible it stays.
Whatever you tell repeatedly your brain starts to believe rapidly!
Like a flame ignited by a matchstick;
Ignite your brain with positive affirmations to align.
Just experiment with these laws of life.
And direct your mind to win and shine!

42. FIND PEACE IN CHAOS

While the world seems busy and noisy all over;
You don't need to run away from the crowd for peace to hover.
Just take few breathes to find your inner peace.
Peace is a valley that is centered within you.
Mind deluding the path to reach.
Coherent connection with the breath within reach.
Trains your brain to feed in pain.
When solitude clings, practice centering your mind.
That builds focusing within you to find the hidden clues.
Centering your mind shall keep the peace within reach.
Even at times of chaos when balance breach.
Keep in mind one fair truth behind.
Absence of noise is not true peace.
Presence of awareness being the only way retreat.

43. THE WAY IS WITHIN YOU

Everything you wish begins within you,
As your inner beauty strengthens and blooms.
No more puzzle pieces scattered ahead.
All at right places in order, at stretch.
Whatever you search is waiting for you.
Deep beneath the silence rests the source of stillness within you.
The way you respond to things around,
Enhances your inner beauty abound.
Everything begins as you step into things.
Instead of overthinking about the happenings.
Step into things as your action begins.
The game of life teaches astound;
The mysteries hidden within your heart abound.

44. THE UNIVERSE

The Universe meaning one single verse.
Dancing gracefully with its cosmic elegance in twirls.
Pulsating between the breath of galaxies and the numerous
creatures.
From the hummingbird to the whale that swirls.
Each movement in nature signifying its resonant feature.
The universe celebrating its every creature.
Echoing the pattern of nature.
In the state of oneness,
A symbolic resonance between the mind and the universe.
Where the mind dissolves in the absence of observance.
Merging with the vast self,
Expanding into the vast oneness of surreal creations!

45. THE COSMIC SONG

Long ago before the words emerged,
The tune of the universe was in breath,
The ripples of water and the oceans hush,
Resonating with human's breath.
As you hear a piece of music,
Not only in the listener's throne,
You get in tune with it, as you feel the rhythm alive
Into your nerves, as the notes rush,
The universe hushing and pulsating inside;
The everlasting cosmic song with rhythm alive!

46. BELIEVE TO HAPPEN

BELIEF is the mantra.
The silent architect behind, all the miracles rush.
Belief being the pure commitment to the soul,
Of the infinite possibilities to explore.
When you begin to truly believe,
The world begins to bend.
To work with the vision, upheld for a mission.
Doors begin to open;
As you start to purely believe.
Belief leads to creation.
You become what you believe.
Things don't happen as you wait,
Change occurs as your heart ripples;
The mantra of belief.
Belief being the seed;
Watering with hopes you proceed!

47. THE PATH OF TRUTH

The most powerful path to walk;
Is to walk on the path of truth.
As it roars, its silent clues.
Clearing away the mental fog;
Directing the way as you walk.
Strengthening your inner voice,
As you travel miles afar.
Building a strong foundational path,
Where nothing collapses apart.
Daring to say what you feel,
Without longing any approval.
Leading your life, the way you believe,
Without trembling out with fears.
Walking in the path of truth;
Strengthens the whole root,
To stand tall still, amidst the chaos around you!

48. LIVE LIFE TO THE FULLEST

Prioritising your "SELF".
You live life to the fullest.
Self-development a journey to discover your potential.
Life cannot bloom without inner groom.
As you deepen inside, you widen outside.
Awakening your purpose,
Knowing your values, mastering your mind,
Practicing new habits that challenge your brain.
You grow and rise above binds,
To give and live.
Wherever there is truth, love nurtures its fruits.
Enjoy the journey of life,
Remembering you are not just the body and mind,
But the pure awareness ever alive behind them!

Epilogue

As you turn this final page, remember this:

Dreams are the sparks that ignite our imagination but it is discipline that keeps the fire burning. This book has not been about becoming perfect, but about becoming intentional. It has not been about blind ambition, but about aligned action. Your future is not built in grand gestures, but in the quiet moments when no one is watching, when you show up, do the work, and keep going. So dream boldly. But more importantly, live with discipline.

Because a disciplined dreamer doesn't just wish. They build !

www.ingramcontent.com/pod-product-compliance
Lightning Source LLC
Chambersburg PA
CBHW020511160726
47991CB00007B/2905